Contents

Contents 1
Introduction 3
Chapter 1 5
Is the espresso business for you? 5
   Determining if you have what it takes.................. 5
Chapter 2 7
How much money will I make? 7
   Illustration 1 Sample Profit and Loss Worksheet..... 8
   Cost of Supplies 12
Chapter 3 15
Getting started 15
   The steps to the road of success 15
   Pitfalls to avoid.. 18
Chapter 4 19
Whether to buy a business or build a business........ 19
   Starting a new drive through espresso stand 20
      Location, Location, Location. 20
      Negotiating a lease 21
      Start up costs 22
      Sample Blueprint 24
      Planning the menu... 26
   Purchasing an existing drive through 28
      How much should you pay for an espresso business?
      28
      Pricing example... 31
      Sample purchase proposal 33
Chapter 5 35
The fundamentals of making espresso drinks 35

Extracting espresso shots	37
Steaming the milk	38
Preparing various drinks	38
Chapter 6	41
Hiring and managing employees	41
Employment Contract	41
Secret shoppers	43
Chapter 7	46
Smooth Operating	46
Chapter 8 Worksheets	47
Drive through espresso location checklist	47
New Employee Checklist	48
Creating a business plan	49
Sample Business Plan	51

Introduction

I have been inspired to write this how-to book after being approached over the years by dozens of people, wondering if they should buy an espresso stand. Does the espresso business have a future? Is this a get rich quick business? How profitable is it? What are the costs involved? Should I buy an existing business? Which coffee should I use? The list of questions is endless. To save you the guesswork and financial mistakes, I have compiled all of my knowledge on the subject into one easy-to-use book. The coffee business, if you do it right, can offer great personal and financial rewards. This book will guide you through the whole process of building or purchasing, and successfully running an espresso stand. If you set yourself up for success from the beginning, your investment of time and money will pay off.

Does this business have a future? From 2000 to 2001 in the U.S., the percentage of 'gourmet' coffee drinkers increased by 57%. In 2001, that strong attraction to specialty coffee exploded into a $6 billion industry (Tea and Coffee Trade Journal, barista primer II). The consumption of espresso based drinks is the fastest growing trend in the U.S, and there is no sign of it slowing down. Taking those statistics into consideration there is definitely potential for growth in any area of the U.S. You can capitalize on that potential if you do your research and put in the time to make sure your business is set up for success.

I have owned and operated an espresso stand in Spokane, Washington for the last eight years. I have also, during those eight years, purchased two additional profitable espresso stands, one with a partner. I currently own two drive through espresso stands. I started both stands without a penny out of my personal financial accounts, and my first business was bought and paid for in less than four years. This book will set your business up to be just as successful. Over the years I have watched many people start their own espresso businesses. Because of lack of proper planning and knowledge, often those businesses failed. So for everyone who wants and needs advice on the subject, here is the complete guide for starting up or purchasing your own drive-through espresso business.

Introduction

I have been inspired to write this how-to book after being approached over the years by dozens of people, wondering if they should buy an espresso stand. Does the espresso business have a future? Is this a get rich quick business? How profitable is it? What are the costs involved? Should I buy an existing business? Which coffee should I use? The list of questions is endless. To save you the guesswork and financial mistakes, I have compiled all of my knowledge on the subject into one easy–to-use book. The coffee business, if you do it right, can offer great personal and financial rewards. This book will guide you through the whole process of building or purchasing, and successfully running an espresso stand. If you set yourself up for success from the beginning, your investment of time and money will pay off.

Does this business have a future? From 2000 to 2001 in the U.S., the percentage of 'gourmet' coffee drinkers increased by 57%. In 2001, that strong attraction to specialty coffee exploded into a $6 billion industry (Tea and Coffee Trade Journal, barista primer II). The consumption of espresso based drinks is the fastest growing trend in the U.S, and there is no sign of it slowing down. Taking those statistics into consideration there is definitely potential for growth in any area of the U.S. You can capitalize on that potential if you do your research and put in the time to make sure your business is set up for success.

I have owned and operated an espresso stand in Spokane, Washington for the last eight years. I have also, during those eight years, purchased two additional profitable espresso stands, one with a partner. I currently own two drive through espresso stands. I started both stands without a penny out of my personal financial accounts, and my first business was bought and paid for in less than four years. This book will set your business up to be just as successful. Over the years I have watched many people start their own espresso businesses. Because of lack of proper planning and knowledge, often those businesses failed. So for everyone who wants and needs advice on the subject, here is the complete guide for starting up or purchasing your own drive-through espresso business.

Chapter 1

Is the espresso business for you?

<u>Determining if you have what it takes</u>
Ask yourself these questions.
1. Am I outgoing, friendly and personable?
2. Could I successfully manage employees, including offering motivation and discipline when necessary?
3. Do I have the money management skills to run a business?
4. Do I have the time, energy, and determination to commit to starting my own business?

Your answers to these questions are very important and they will determine the success of your coffee business.
1. In the drive-through coffee business you will come into contact with many people from diverse social groups and backgrounds. It is your job to appeal to all customers regardless of social status, and to train your employees to do the same. Every customer should feel welcome and taken care of. A business where the owner is involved gives customers the feeling of a personal touch. People like to see whom their business is supporting, and if you are not friendly or personable with them, then they will take their business elsewhere. In some cases, you are the first person your customers see and talk to during their day. Your thoughtful interactions can set the tone for their entire day! Also, the tone that *you* set in your workplace is the tone which your employees will adopt in your absence. Unless you want to work all the time, your business is dependent on the performance of your employees.

2. Remember the Golden Rule: "treat your employees as you would want to be treated." Intentionally or otherwise, your staff will inform your customers of the kind of manager or boss that you are. Your employees will build rapport with their customers, and your employees will pass your treatment of them on to your customers. Do you treat your employees with respect? Do you treat them all fairly? Do you try to be accommodating to their schedule requests? Do you have the ability to confront and discipline if necessary? The respect that you give your employees will show through in their work ethic and customer service. Once you build a reliable staff and have established rapport with them, then your hours can be reduced since they will treat the business as if it was their own and take care of the customers as you would.
3. Drive-through espresso is a cash business. If you are not disciplined in monitoring the cash flow it is easy to over-extend yourself. If you are someone who does not have a good concept of money management, then maybe owning your own business is not your best option. If you lack money management skills and still dream of owning your own business, then work closely with an accountant to stay on top of your expenses.
4. Owning your own business has many benefits, such as setting your own hours and being your own boss. Once it is up and running an espresso stand can be very profitable for the number of hours that you have to put in. However, setting your business up for success takes a lot of time and energy. Choosing the perfect location, building a new stand, building rapport with customers, marketing your product, and training yourself and your staff are all very important factors in the success of your business. Make sure that the timing is right for you and that you are ready to take on the challenge.

Chapter 2

How much money will I make?

This is easily the question that I am asked most frequently and the one that is the hardest to answer. Your profit will equal roughly 20% of your yearly gross sales. There is no set limit to your income potential. It will depend greatly on your location, product, and service. Using the following monthly profit and loss worksheets as your guide (Illustrations 1, 2, 3), you can get an idea of your expected profits. Be sure to change the variables to fit your situation, such as monthly sales, rent, loan payment, and payroll. If your location is not ideal, you will not operate at a profit; instead you will merely be buying yourself a minimum wage job, as shown in illustration 3. These profit and loss statements are great tools to use when purchasing an existing business. They allow you to predict your potential profit and the kind of financial rewards you can expect as you gain more customers. However, when starting a business with no customer base, these profits are "blue sky." Blue Sky is the business term that is used for the number of customers that you hope to obtain or the customer base that an existing business already has in place. When you purchase an existing customer base there is no guarantee that those customers will stay with you through the change of ownership. In the Spokane market where I live, many new businesses, placed on busy streets with easy accessibility and consistently good service have grossed over $160,000.00 a year from the start. From there those businesses have continued to grow year after year. You never know what your actual profit potential will be in starting up a new business until you take the chance and start. Once you have followed all of the steps in this book and have taken the necessary steps to ensure your success, you can feel confident that your investment of time and money will pay off.

Illustration 1 Sample Profit and Loss Worksheet
Gross yearly sales $185,000.00 approximately 229 customers daily

Gross Monthly Sales (based on $514.00 day)	$15,400.00
Cost of Goods Sold (the cost of all products used to make your drinks: coffee, syrup, cups, etc.) Approximately 32% of gross sales.	$ 4,928.00
Gross Monthly Profit	$10,472.00
Additional Expenses	
Rent (payment for leased land your stand is on)	$ 1,100.00
Loan Payment (bank, owner contract, note payable, credit card etc.)	$ 1,200.00
Electricity	$ 175.00
Water, Garbage, Recycling	$ 120.00
Payroll (based on 16 hours/ day hired out @ $7.01 hour)	$ 3364.80
Payroll taxes (SS and Medicare; 7.65% of gross payroll)	$ 257.41
Unemployment taxes (payable quarterly) approx.	$ 75.00
L&I insurance (payable quarterly) approx.	$ 60.00
B&O taxes (gross sales x .00471)	$ 72.53
Repairs and Maintenance	$ 100.00
Insurance	$ 60.00
Telephone	$ 50.00
Office Supplies	$ 35.00
Accounting	$ 50.00
Misc. supplies	$ 75.00
Licenses (renewable yearly at $286.00)	$ 24.00
Total addition expenses	$ 6,818.74
Monthly net (profit)	$ 3653.26

Illustration2 Sample Profit and Loss Worksheet
Gross yearly sales $150,000.00 approximately 185 Customers a day

Gross Monthly Sales (based on $416.00 day)	$12,500.00
Cost of Goods Sold (the cost of all products used to make your drinks: coffee, syrup, cups, etc.) Approximately 32% of gross sales.	$ 4,000.00
Gross Monthly Profit	$ 8,500.00
Additional Expenses	
Rent (payment for leased land your stand is on)	$ 1,100.00
Loan Payment (bank, owner contract, note payable, credit card etc.)	$ 1,200.00
Electricity	$ 175.00
Water, Garbage, Recycling	$ 120.00
Payroll (based on 16 hours/ day hired out @ $7.01 hour)	$ 3364.80
Payroll taxes (SS and Medicare; 7.65% of gross payroll)	$ 257.41
Unemployment taxes (payable quarterly) approx.	$ 75.00
L&I insurance (payable quarterly) approx.	$ 60.00
B&O taxes (gross sales x .00471)	$ 72.53
Repairs and Maintenance	$ 100.00
Insurance	$ 60.00
Telephone	$ 50.00
Office Supplies	$ 35.00
Accounting	$ 50.00
Misc. supplies	$ 75.00
Licenses (renewable yearly at $286.00)	$ 24.00
Total addition expenses	$ 6,818.74
Monthly net (profit)	$ 1681.26

Illustration 3 Sample Profit and Loss Worksheet
Gross yearly sales $120,000.00 approximately 150 customers daily

Gross Monthly Sales (based on $333.00 day)	$10,000.00
Cost of Goods Sold (the cost of all products used to make your drinks: coffee, syrup, cups, etc.) Approximately 32% of gross sales.	$ 3,200.00
Gross Monthly Profit	$ 6,800.00
Additional Expenses	
Rent (payment for leased land your stand is on)	$ 1,100.00
Loan Payment (bank, owner contract, note payable, credit card etc.)	$ 1,200.00
Electricity	$ 175.00
Water, Garbage, Recycling	$ 120.00
Payroll (based on 16 hours/ day hired out @ $7.01 hour)	$ 3364.80
Payroll taxes (SS and Medicare; 7.65% of gross payroll)	$ 257.41
Unemployment taxes (payable quarterly) approx.	$ 75.00
L&I insurance (payable quarterly) approx.	$ 60.00
B&O taxes (gross sales x .00471)	$ 72.53
Repairs and Maintenance	$ 100.00
Insurance	$ 60.00
Telephone	$ 50.00
Office Supplies	$ 35.00
Accounting	$ 50.00
Misc. supplies	$ 75.00
Licenses (renewable yearly at $286.00)	$ 24.00
Total addition expenses	$ 6,818.74
Monthly net (profit)	($ -18.74)

In all of these examples the variables are based on taxes and wages in the Spokane market. Review your city's Business and Occupation tax rate and your state's industrial insurance and unemployment insurance, as those rates will vary.

A loan of $60,000.00 at 7.5 % interest would be repaid in five years with monthly loan payments of $1202.28. When that loan is paid in full your monthly profit will increase by the amount of your loan payment. In these examples that loan payment is $1200.00 per month.

Cost of Supplies
This worksheet represents the price per unit of items used in preparing each drink. Using this guide and revising it to fit your costs will give you your percentage of cost of goods sold.

Milk
Chocolate $2.70
Whole $2.25
Skim $1.85
Average $2.27 gallon
1 gallon of milk 128 oz.
cost of milk per drink: 13 oz milk for iced 20 oz. Drink $0.23
                       16 oz milk for hot 20 oz. Drink $0.28

Syrup
Torani 25 oz. bottle $3.99
Per oz $0.16
Cost of syrup per drink: 2oz syrup $0.32

Coffee
Whole bean coffee per lb. $5.75
cost of 1 shot $0.13
*45 shots per pound

Cups
20 oz. Paper cup $0.10
20 oz. Plastic cup $0.09

Lids
20 oz. Paper Cup lid $0.02
20 oz. Clear Plastic lid $0.02

Straws
Hot drink cocktail straw $0.005
Iced drink 8" (fat) $0.006

Labels
Custom printed drink labels $0.03

Total Cost Per Drink

20 oz hot latte double with flavor		20 oz iced latte double with flavor	
Coffee (2 shot)	$0.26	Coffee (2 shot)	$0.26
Milk (16 oz.)	$0.28	Milk (13 oz.)	$0.23
Syrup (2 oz.)	$0.32	Syrup (2 oz.)	$0.32
Cup (20 oz.)	$0.10	Cup (20 oz.)	$0.09
Lid	$0.02	Lid	$0.02
Straw	$0.01	Straw	$0.01
Label	$0.03	Label	$0.03
Total	$1.02	Total	$0.96

If a 20-oz. double flavored latte is $3.25 and your cost to make it is $1.02, then your cost of goods sold percentage would be 31%. (This calculation is done by taking the cost of the drink and dividing it by the cost it is sold for $1.02 ÷ $3.25 = .31)

There are many variables here. If you use chocolate milk in your mochas, put whip cream on your drinks, or double cup when using hot paper cups, then your cost of goods will be higher.

Chapter 3

Getting started

Now that you have made the decision to invest the time and money to start your own drive through espresso stand, here is what you need to do for ensured success, do not skip <u>any</u> of the following steps.

<u>The steps to the road of success</u>

1. <u>Start a business strategy or plan</u>. There are many agencies available at little or no cost to help you design a business plan. The Small Business Administration and the Business Development Center are two resources available in Washington State. They can help you with all aspects of starting a business, such as expected start-up costs, budgeting, expected profits, and financing. Use the worksheet and example at the back of the book to aid you in developing your business plan.
2. <u>Check with your city's building and zoning department</u> to see if drive through espresso stands are allowed. In some parts of the country, drive through espresso is a foreign concept. Set up an appointment and bring with you pictures, plans, and an ideal location where you want to operate. The more information you bring to the table, the better idea they will have of what you are trying to accomplish.
3. <u>Find the best location possible</u>. This cannot be stressed enough---location, location, location. The location of your drive through is the single most important factor in ensuring success. Your location will make or break you. The ideal location is on a highly visible street where access to your stand is easy. Easy access includes turning into your business as well as exiting back into the flow of traffic. The most

desirable locations are close to a college campus, near a large housing development or apartment complex, or on a busy street with 35,000 cars or more per day.
4. Get your finances in order. There are many ways to obtain money to buy or build an espresso stand. The options include a small business loan, home equity loans, personal lines of credit, owner financing, or family and friends. When you have a business plan and a successful location secured, financing should not be an issue.
5. Negotiate a lease. Again, choosing a location is the single most important decision that you will make. Do not let the price of the land lease affect your decision. If you have an excellent location, then you can easily afford a $1000.00 -$2000.00 lease payment per month. It is far better to pay for the perfect location and make money, than to save money by leasing a cheaper spot and sacrificing earning potential. Only the *conditions* of the lease should affect your decision. I always advise against a month to month lease. In the Spokane market monthly rent payments run from $300.00 per month to $1800.00 per month, with the average approximating $850.00. A safe lease would be an agreement where your rent is no more than 8% of your gross sales and the term is at least five years. For example, if your gross monthly sales are $15,000.00, negotiate your monthly lease not to exceed $1200.00. If you are looking to purchase an existing stand, 5%-7% of the current gross sales (taken from the last years tax returns), because your investment will be more than if you were starting your own (you are buying their customer base). If their last year's gross sales were $185,000.00, Re negotiate the lease to between $750.00 and $1000.00 per month. This will ensure that you recuperate your investment in a timely manner. (Refer to profit and loss, illustration 1, based on these numbers).
6. Find a local coffee roasting company to work with. Meet with several different roasters and make your decision according to how willing

they are to help you during your new business planning. You have to love the coffee that you are selling otherwise you will not be passionate about your product. Your enthusiasm for your produt will be passed onto your employees and customers. Your roaster can be a great asset to you at this time, finding a perfect espresso blend for you, assisting with training, promotions, building design and layout, and equipment purchasing.

7. <u>Start your training</u>. If you do not have experience in the espresso field, now is the time to start increasing your knowledge and training. The first place to look is your local coffee roasting company. Many companies will extensively train you and your staff at no charge. Why? Because if you use their product and you are successful, they too make money. They have an investment in your business.

    Here is another option: If you know someone in the business, you could pay him or her to train you. However, your training is then limited to their level of knowledge and relies on the assumption that they were trained properly. Other options are "How-To" videos sold on the Internet, hands on training done by coffee product suppliers, or at coffee conventions. This book contains the basic terminology and training tips, but these alone are not enough to start your own business. You need hands on training for a minimum of two weeks before serving your first customer. Remember: first impressions are lasting ones.

8. <u>Start construction plans,</u> emphasizing a design that will serve your customers in the fastest and most efficient manner. Pay close attention to equipment layout. A commercial espresso or specialty restaurant supply company can help with the layout to maximize your efficiency in preparing drinks and serving customers.

9. <u>Set up an appointment with an accountant</u> to determine your bookkeeping and tax responsibilities. Your accountant can help you

decide whether to take these duties on yourself or hire an accountant or bookkeeper to perform these tasks.

Pitfalls to avoid

From being in the business for several years, making mistakes and learning from them I have discovered some pitfalls to avoid:

1. <u>Partnerships</u> can seem like the solution to a business venture. There are two people to share the work load, financial responsibility, book work, and errands. The down sides of a partnership are that there are two people that have to agree on when they want to work, how they want to spend money, which of you is to do the errands and how the business is going to be run. I call business partnerships a marriage based on money. It is a successful relationship for some, but it takes good communication skills, and sharing common goals and ideas. I have been involved in one partnership and even though I really liked and respected my partner it was still more difficult to run that business than to run the other two businesses on my own.
2. <u>Written Contracts</u> are a must. Something agreed to verbally between two people is not binding. A contract signed between two people is necessary whenever business is transacted. Never enter into any agreement until you fully understand all aspects involved, whether it is a lease, vendor contract, or sale.

Chapter 4

Whether to buy a business or build a business

There are a couple of factors you must consider before choosing the avenue that is right for you and your drive through espresso business.

1. Evaluate your city's current coffee situation. Are there already too many existing drive through espresso stands in your area? Are all of the profitable, ideal locations taken? If so, trying to compete with up and running stands with an established customer base may limit your potential if you build another drive through. Purchasing one of the stands that is already up and running rather than pulling from their customer base, would be the safe way to go, only if your area is already too over-populated with drive through espresso stands. The ideal purchase would be one where the potential business is there, but the business is not being operated properly. Due to poor customer service, inconsistent drinks, or poor money management. These businesses are the best ones to take over because you are not paying for the customers that are already there, you are banking on the fact that you can run the business better and attract more customers. This is usually the case with a good location that is lacking strong ownership. However, if the proper location is available to start your own drive through it is generally wiser instead of purchasing someone else's problem.
2. Consider the time that you want to invest. Are you looking for a full time job? Or are you looking to make money putting in as few hours as possible? Getting a new espresso stand up and running takes a lot of research, planning and time. Starting a new business and building up the clientele will take up much of your time. Plan on putting in at least

40 hours a week for the first six months. This does not include all of the planning, research, and building prior to opening your stand. On the other hand an existing espresso stand with established clientele and trained employees would take up less of your time. However, you will pay for that clientele base and those trained employees. Remember that each city has the potential for growth in the drive through espresso business. You just need to take the avenue that is right for you and it is going to depend on the situation in *your* city. Do your research on locations and traffic count to find the best business location available, whether it is an existing business or a new location.

Starting a new drive through espresso stand

Location, Location, Location.

This is the single most important decision that you will make when starting your drive through espresso business. Use the location checklist at the back of the book to ensure the key factors for selecting a location are not overlooked.

The best places for drive through espresso stands are:
- College towns or near a college campus
- In the downtown central business district
- Strip malls or gas station parking lots

Ideally place your stand on the side of the street with high-traffic or major commuter thoroughfares with easy re entry to traffic, the side of the street that cars pass while going to work. The morning traffic commuters are your customers. Make sure the location is highly visible (commuters can see it before they drive past) and easily accessible. A large reader board to attract customers and an easily accessible stand will positively affect your business. Again, it is better to pay $2000.00 per month for a location that will show you a profit, than $500.00 per month for a spot where you will lose money. If you are unsure of a good location, work closely with a licensed Realtor in your city to find the ideal property. There is no charge to use a Realtor and he or she often can be a great asset in your search. Last, remember to check with your city's zoning department that the property that you want to lease is properly zoned for drive through espresso.

Let's look again at my hometown as an example. The population within the city limits is approximately 200,000 people. There are over 50 drive through espresso stands, numerous walk in coffee shops, and over 17 Starbuck's locations all located within the city limits. In my opinion, Spokane is saturated with drive through stands, but there are still ideal locations available here. I believe there are numerous locations throughout the U.S. where a drive through espresso stand operation would thrive. If the city of Spokane can support this many coffee vendors, your City can as well. Do your research, set up an ideal location, receive the proper training, and you can reap the rewards of owning your own drive through espresso stand.

Negotiating a lease

Once you have found the ideal location, it is time to contact the property owner and negotiate a lease. Remember, it is better to pay more and make a profit than to pay less and lose money. Make sure that you negotiate a lease for the length of time that it will take you to recover your investment. I recommend at least a five-year lease with the option to renew at the end of the lease term. I also recommend paying an attorney to review the lease to make sure that you are entering into the lease fully knowledgeable and understanding of all the contents included in the lease agreement.

Start up costs

The start up cost of building an espresso stand has many variables. The example below is based on start up costs in Spokane, WA. Local building codes vary greatly from city to city and state to state. Your first step in this process, before you build, is to obtain a list of policies from your city planning department this will enable you to determine the codes, zoning requirements, permits, and special requirements you will have to meet in order to open and operate your drive- through espresso.

a. A standard sized espresso stand is approximately 20ft long by 10ft wide with a drive through window on each side, it contains the following equipment: a two or three group espresso machine, two grinders, a double barrel granita machine, a soft serve ice cream machine, a double sided sliding door refrigerator, an under cabinet refrigerator, an automatic ice machine, a commercial blender, a cash register, a three compartment sink, a mop sink, and possibly a bathroom. Without a bathroom this package will cost approximately $45,000.00. Putting a bathroom in the stand will increase the building price approximately $5,000.00.

b. Here is a breakdown of costs: (for a middle of the line stand)
   1. Building permits, water and power hook-ups, foundation, structure, widows, cabinets, shelving, and flooring.
   2. Building 10 ft. wide by 20 ft. long, built by an independent contractor will cost around $24,000, approximately $29,000 with a bathroom.
   3. Equipment:

Two group espresso machine	$6,000.00
Double sided glass refrigerator	$2,000.00
Two grinders	$1,500.00
Double-barrel granita machine	$3,000.00
Soft serve ice cream machine	$3,000.00
Automatic Ice machine	$1,800.00

Under cabinet refrigerator	$ 800.00
Vita Mix commercial blender	$ 400.00
Cash register	$ 150.00
4. Starting inventory	$1,500.00
5. Cash in till	$ 150.00

- Site improvements could result in additional costs. Examples of these are: hooking up to city sewer and water, paving the site parking lot, connecting the electricity, building permits, and required landscape. These could increase the cost by as much as $20,000.00. Do your research ahead of time to know your expenses going in.

Sample Blueprint

Below is a blueprint of an average sized espresso stand that is 10'x 20'.

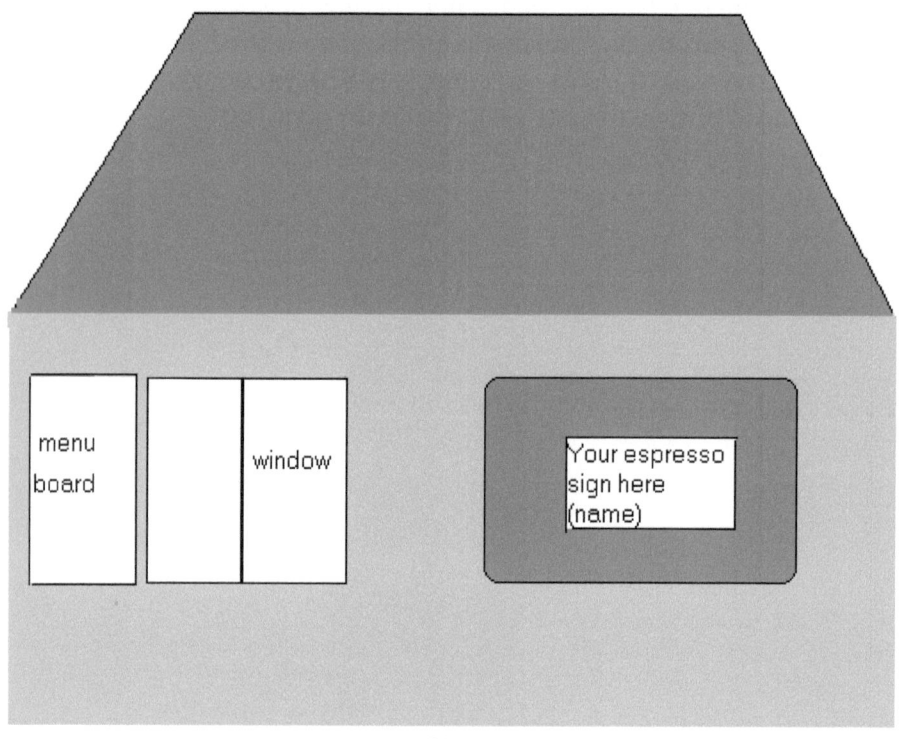

Interior view

Here is a very functional layout for fast and efficient service. Please note there are drive-through windows on each side. Also, under the espresso machine is an under cabinet refrigerator. There are garbage cans under the counter on each side of the espresso machine for your coffee grounds to be knocked into. As your business increases you may want to place another cash register on the counter above the ice machine to get customers through more efficiently. Remember that experienced roasters or commercial restaurant suppliers will help with layout design before construction begins. Proper equipment layout is a key factor in fast, efficient customer service.

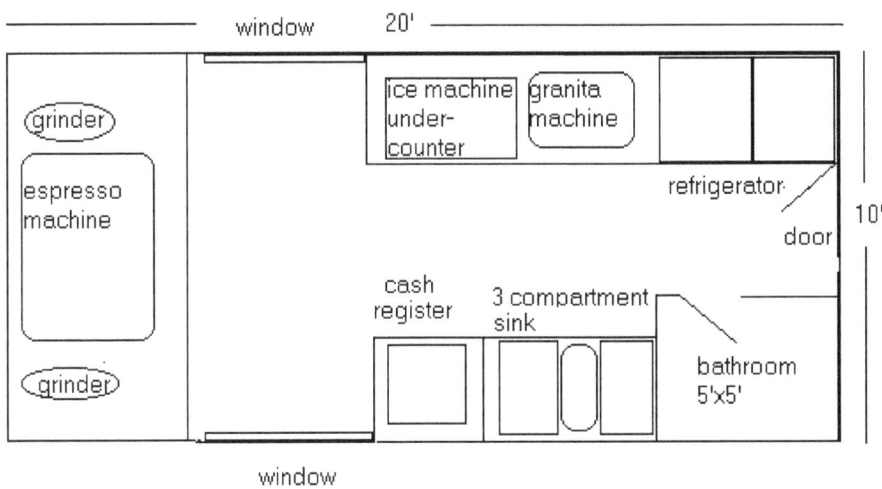

Planning the menu

Planning the menu design and layout is something that many business owners overlook or save until the last minute. My advice is to keep it simple. Use a material for your menu board that will withstand exterior weather conditions and will not warp. Also use a material such as vinyl for the letters and numbers so that you can peel them off to change prices without having to have new menu boards made. Make sure that your drinks are competitively priced for your areas coffee market. Compare your prices with the local competition. For my menu I chose to include a brief description of the drink to aid the customer in ordering. To speed up the cash handling, price your drinks at twenty-five cent increments, and include tax in your prices. Below is a sample menu the prices are current based on the Northwest's coffee market.

(Your business name here)

	12oz	16oz	20oz	32oz
Espresso	1.50			
Strong, straight, and simple				
Americano	1.50	1.50	1.50	1.75
Espresso diluted with hot water				
Cappuccino	2.25	2.50	2.75	4.00
Espresso & creamy froth				
Latte	2.25	2.50	2.75	4.00
Espresso & steamed milk				
Breve	2.50	2.75	3.00	4.25
Espresso, & steamed half and half				
Mocha	2.50	2.75	3.00	4.25
Espresso, steamed milk, & Chocolate syrup				
Granita	2.50	2.75	3.00	4.25
Our own special recipe!				
Chai	2.50	2.75	3.00	4.25
A delicious blend of Black tea, honey, ginger, and other spices				
Hot Chocolate	1.50	1.75	2.00	3.25
Hershey's & steamed milk, topped With whip cream				
Jet Tea or X-treme Smoothies	2.75	3.00	3.25	4.25
Espresso Shake	2.75	3.00	3.25	4.25
Ice cream & coffee blended				
Italian Soda	1.75	2.00	2.25	3.50
Italian syrup & club soda Topped with whip cream				
Iced Tea & Lemonade	1.50	1.75	2.00	3.00

Purchasing an existing drive through

Now that you have an idea of the cost to build and open your own espresso stand, let's look at purchasing an existing, operating drive through espresso business.

Drive through espresso stands are plentiful in the northwest where I live and in many other areas of the country. If you are looking to get into the espresso business there are advantages to purchasing an existing stand. Before you do, however, you should do your homework and research the business to know exactly what you are buying. A stand in a highly visible location with easy access and the potential to grow is ideal. If the stand is currently not being run properly by its owner, the profits and customer base will be low relative to its potential. In both cases where I purchased an existing stand, the owners were not very involved in their business and employees had a negative attitude toward their owners and their job. That attitude was passed on to the customers. There was also product waste and lack of accountability in both inventory and cash flow. During my first year of ownership all of my businesses' sales increased over 20% and continued to grow from there. There is always room for growth in the drive through business. Unless there are cars driving away because the wait in line is too long, the business can accommodate a larger customer base. With the proper tools and training you can purchase an existing business and reach its full potential.

How much should you pay for an espresso business?

When you are looking to purchase a stand there are three major factors that determine whether or not the stand will be profitable:
- The purchase price and current value of assets
- Transferring or renegotiating a lease
- Expected profits based on past performance

1. A rough guide for estimating the purchase price of an existing drive through business is 50% of their last full year's gross sales. For example, if an existing business showed $150,000.00 in gross sales on their last year's tax return, the asking price could be about $75,000.00. On average the stands in my area (depending on the condition of the stand, equipment and fixtures) sell for approximately 40% of their gross yearly sales, so that number is definitely negotiable. Is the purchase price more than the value of assets (such as building, equipment, and inventory)? The dollar amount that you pay in excess of the value of the assets is called blue sky, goodwill, or customer base. If you take over ownership are the customers going to stay with you? In all three of my purchases, from existing owners the business not only stayed, but also increased over 20% the first year. The customer base in all of my purchases made them worth buying. However, paying too much for the "blue sky" could make the business less profitable because of the increased loan payments. This is where it pays to find a business that is not as profitable, but has great growth potential because of the mistakes the current owner is making. You must also weigh all of the factors affecting your purchase such as monthly lease, lease term, and the potential for customer growth. If you are buying a building that is considerably nicer than other drive-through stands, the asking price will be higher. But, even if the existing owner has spent $100,000 fixing it up, it is worth no more to you unless it gives you room to expand the customer base with such things as indoor seating, a walk up window, or an additional drive up window. Just because the building is large or expensively done does not mean that its location is going to support those expenses. Make sure to pay for their customer base, not just the building. Unless you are purchasing the land that the

building is on, the building should not be a significant contributing factor to price.
2. I would not purchase an existing stand unless the lease will extend to me for the same amount of time that it would take me to pay off the business. Here is an example: I am considering purchasing a stand and the lease is only two years. I purchase this business for $50,000.00. I put 20% down and borrow the rest from the bank. After two years I still owe approximately $30,000.00, and my equipment has depreciated. If my lease is not extended at the end of the two years, I now have to pick up and move and start over with a new client base. That customer base that I am buying is no good unless I have the extended lease to back it up. Also, make sure that you thoroughly read the lease agreement and that this lease is transferable. Contact the landowner and speak to them personally, about your interest in purchasing the business. This again will ensure that the seller is communicating the proper lease information, such as monthly rent, lease term, transferability, or any additional expenses involved in renting this property. If necessary re-negotiate the lease with the landowner and make your purchase agreement with the seller contingent on your lease terms being met.
3. Base your offer on past performance. Use the owner's past Department of Revenue (sales tax) and Federal Tax returns to determine daily or yearly sales. To determine the profit at which this business is operating and the profits you can expect use the profit and loss illustrations provided adjusting the figures according to sales and expenses. You do not want to be buying yourself a job. If you have to work 30-40 hours per week to make $20,000.00 a year, then this stand is not for you. The right one will come along if you are diligent and patient.

Pricing example

Here is an example of what an existing drive through espresso stand should sell for, based on the profit and loss illustration, assets, and transferable lease.

This example would be a great purchase opportunity only if it had the traffic to build the customer base (over 35,000 cars on its street per day). Remember, location, location, location. Customers will not go out of their way to come to you.

Sample Profit and Loss Worksheet (gross sales $120,000.00; 150 customers daily)

Current Gross Monthly Sales (based on $333.00 day)	$10,000.00
Cost of Goods Sold (the cost of all products used to make your drinks: coffee, syrup, cups, etc.) Approximately 32% of gross sales.	$ 3,200.00
Gross Monthly Profit	$ 6,800.00
Additional Expenses	
Rent (payment for leased land your stand is on)	$ 800.00
Loan Payment (bank, owner contract, note payable, credit card etc.)	$ 1,200.00
Electricity	$ 175.00
Water, Garbage, Recycling	$ 120.00
Payroll (based on 16 hours /day hired out @ $7.01 hour)	$ 3364.80
Payroll taxes (SS and Medicare; 7.65% of gross payroll)	$ 257.41
Unemployment taxes (payable quarterly) approx.	$ 75.00
L&I insurance (payable quarterly) approx.	$ 60.00
B&O taxes (gross sales x .00471)	$ 72.53
Repairs and Maintenance	$ 100.00
Insurance	$ 60.00
Telephone	$ 50.00
Office Supplies	$ 35.00
Accounting	$ 50.00
Misc. supplies	$ 75.00
Licenses (renewable yearly at $286.00)	$ 24.00
Total addition expenses	$ 6,518.74

| Monthly net (profit) | $ 218.26 |

      A fair purchase price for this example would be $40,000.00 to $60,000.00.

The reasons that this stand would be worth this amount to you as a purchaser:

- You would have a five-year lease during which time the revenue generated from sales would pay for the purchase of the espresso stand.
- It would cost you approximately $45,000.00 to build a new stand. If this stand is relatively new and still in good condition, then you are paying about $15,000.00 for their established customer base and saving yourself all of the time and trouble of constructing a new stand and building your business from scratch.
- If the stand is older and run down, then your offer should be on the low end. If the stand is five years old or newer, and in nice condition, then your offer should be on the high end.
- Increasing the sales by only 15% would bring your profit up to $1,301.00 a month. A 30% raise in sales would increase your monthly profit to $2,322.00. Also, take into consideration that once the business is paid for your profit will increase further in the amount of your loan payment. In this example, at that point you would gain an additional $1,200.00 per month.
- After five years you would then have an investment that is paid for in full and worth more than the purchase price because you have increased sales and built a reliable customer base.

Sample purchase proposal

Here is a sample of an actual proposal for the purchase of an espresso stand in the Spokane area.

To <u>(Sellers name here)</u>
Offer for Purchase of (Name of Business)
From (<u>Your name here</u>)

Offer Price: $60,000.00

*Terms: $20,000.00 down and owner carries the contract for the remaining $40,000.00.
*Terms of Contract: 54 months at 8% interest. No prepayment penalty.
*Payments due monthly in the amount of $890.00, due on the 1st of the month.
*First Payment will be due on January 1st, 2001, assuming the stand is purchased on December 1st, 2000.

Reasons for offering price
1) <u>Average Daily Sales for 2000</u> after going over your Ledger for the year 2000, for the first 10 months of business the average daily Sales were approximately $478.00. This means you are on track to do approximately $173,000.00 for the year in 2000. (These are Gross sales, sales tax included.). The slower months of November and December are not included in this average.
2) <u>The condition of the stand on the inside.</u> The countertop, floor, various shelves, etc. need to be replaced. There are holes in the wall in several places.
3) <u>The condition of the equipment</u>. The equipment is all more than five years old and repairs and maintenance have been neglected. The Rio machine needs maintenance. The Taylor soft serve machine needs either maintenance or repaired on one side (it is not freezing the product). We would need to purchase additional equipment such as another refrigerator, another grinder, and a granita machine.
4) <u>Cost of lot rent.</u> Lot rent is currently at $1300.00 a month. It increases at a rate of 1.5% to 3% annually, based on the cost of living increase.

<u>Please contact me with any questions or concerns that you might have with this offer.</u>

This offer is contingent on verification of your 1999 tax return, as well as your Washington State retail sales tax returns for the Year 2000 1st, 2nd and 3rd Quarter verifying sales are the same or <u>more</u> than those on the ledger averaging approx. $478.00 daily for the year 2000.

We appreciate the opportunity to do business with you and anticipate hearing back from you soon.

Sincerely,
(Your name and signature)

This offer was the actual proposal used when negotiating the purchase of a business. The asking price was $90,000. The price paid was $65,000.00.

Chapter 5

The fundamentals of making espresso drinks

Now that you have completed the necessary research to start your own stand or to purchase a drive-through espresso business, it is now time to learn the fundamentals of preparing espresso based drinks.

The best espresso stands are ones in which the owners or managers are knowledgeable of their product. The best way to be knowledgeable is to be a coffee drinker yourself. The term "espresso" is used in regard to the process of brewing coffee. It is the process of hot, pressurized water being forced through finely ground coffee to create what is called an espresso shot. There are several factors that affect the quality of the brewing process of extracting a shot. The five major concerns are <u>coffee freshness</u>, <u>grinding</u>, <u>dosing and tamping</u>, <u>water temperature and purity</u>, and <u>length of shot extraction</u>.

1. <u>Coffee freshness</u>. Coffee should be delivered to you at a minimum of once a week and should come in a sealed valve coffee bag. This bag lets the gas from the roasted coffee escape without allowing any air or oxygen in. Your coffee should be stored in a cool, dry place, off of the floor and away from any products that can contaminate it, such as cleaning products.
2. <u>Grinding your whole bean coffee</u>. This is a major part of properly extracting espresso shots. The ability to adjust the grind properly can be the difference between success and failure in your business. The grind is very temperamental and should be adjusted throughout the day to ensure proper coffee particle size. The grinding burrs in your grinder finely cut and shave the coffee into similar size particles, and that particle size determines how fast the water is poured through the

coffee filter (called a portafilter). The larger the particle size, the faster the water will flow through. The finer the particle size, the slower the coffee will pour through. Controlling the extraction is the single most important factor in determining taste. If the grind is too coarse, the water will flow through too quickly, making your shot under extracted, weak and watery. If the grind is too fine, your shot will be over-extracted, causing your shot to taste burnt and bitter. The perfectly set grind that is tamped properly will extract a shot in from 18 to 24 seconds, and that shot will taste sweet and smooth. I cannot stress enough how this will affect your business. Once coffee is ground it must be used immediately; never pre-grind coffee before it is to be used in a shot. Coffee will lose its flavor characteristics within thirty minutes of being ground. Coffee consumers are becoming more educated and aware of the taste of properly prepared drinks. If your shots are not good, then your drink is not good, and your customers will take their business elsewhere. Monitoring your employees and their ability to adjust the grind to create the perfect shot will be your biggest challenge. Employees may get careless, distracted, or in a hurry and use shots that are not extracted properly, which will result in lost business. It is your job to monitor their performance and train them properly on this technique.

3. Dosing and tamping. Dosing is the amount of ground coffee used to brew the espresso. Filling your portafilter with the correct amount of ground coffee is the next crucial element. The best way is to over fill the portafilter with the ground coffee, then run your finger or a flat utensil over the top of it, disposing of the excess grounds to get a full even dose. Tamping is applying pressure to compact the coffee particles so that the surface is smooth, flat and even, ensuring that the water is filtered through evenly, extracting a perfect shot. Tamping is a two step process. The first step is to place the tamper on the portafilter evenly with your arm at a 90° angle. Apply 30-40 pounds of

pressure (You can practice pressing on your bathroom scale to get a feel for the force required for 30-40 pounds. Also, bring this in as a training aid). Make sure to press with firm even pressure. The second step is to tap the portafilter lightly using the back of the tamper; this will cause any grounds from the inner rim of the portafilter to fall onto the tamped surface. Next with a light pressure place the tamper on the grounds and give a light even twist. This will create what is called a polish. A polish helps to create that smooth even surface for the water to pour through.

4. <u>Water temperature and purity</u>. Coffee is made up of 95% water. Water is a vital component in determining how your drinks will taste. The proper brewing temperature for espresso is between 198 and 202 ° F. Water below this temperature will not extract the full flavor from the shot. While water above 202° will cause your shot to taste burnt. Also of equal importance is the purity of the water. You must install a proper water filtration system with a water purification system. This will ensure proper tasting espresso shots as well as increase the life of your espresso machine. Bad tasting water makes bad tasting shots. If you use unfiltered water in your machine, the minerals and calcium will build up and cause what is called scaling. Scaling is a rocklike substance that builds up in your machine and coats the inside, which lowers the capacity of the boiler in your machine. It may also coat the heating element, affecting the quality of your espresso shots.

5. <u>Length of extraction</u>. The length of time that a shot should pour for is 18-24 seconds, filling a one-ounce shot glass.

Extracting espresso shots

     A correctly extracted shot should fill your shot glass like warm honey. The color should be dark brown on the bottom and towards the top create a silky tan caramel color. The top of the shot (approximately the top third) should be what is called crème. It is a foamy milky substance that tops a perfectly prepared espresso shot. Remember to adjust your grind often to keep your shots within the 18-24 second range.

Steaming the milk

There are two stages to proper milk steaming: foaming and blending. Foaming is the process of injecting air into the milk. Blending mixes the foam with the milk to create a creamy texture.

Proper Foaming. First fill your milk pitcher with only as much milk needed to make the drink. Lower the steam wand deep into the milk just above the bottom of the pitcher. Turn the steam valve on completely and raise the wand slowly so that the tip is just breaking the surface of the milk. You should hear a light hissing sound. This is injecting air into the milk and should be done until the temperature reaches 100°F.

Blending. Now that you have reached 100°F you can start the blending process. Lower the wand deep into the pitcher just above the bottom and tilt the pitcher so that it is at a slight angle. You will continue steaming until the milk temperature reaches 160°F. Make sure that you turn off the steam wand while it is still in the pitcher of milk, then promptly remove it from the steamed milk. Placing the pitcher on the counter, give it a few hard flat taps against the counter top. This will settle any remaining bubbles left on the surface. You should now have a creamy, frothy pitcher of steamed milk to prepare your drink.

Preparing various drinks

Now that you know how to properly extract espresso shots and prepare the milk, let's go through the "how- to's" of making the most common drinks.

Americano: An americano is straight espresso diluted with hot water. It tastes very similar to brewed coffee. The customer controls how strong this drink is by how many shots of espresso go into the drink. If a customer were to request a strong americano, I suggest a double shot of espresso in no larger than a 12oz cup. Always ask customers who order this if they would like cream or sweetener. Correct preparation is pouring the espresso shots into the cup, then adding hot water to the top.

Latte: A latte consists of straight shots of espresso and steamed milk. Your most requested drinks will be flavored lattes. Here is the correct preparation of this drink: Place a measured ounce of syrup into the bottom of the cup, then pour in your shots of espresso. Stir to blend the flavor and coffee. Then slowly add the creamy steamed milk.

Mocha: A mocha is the same concept as a flavored latte, except that you are using chocolate syrup for the flavor. Stir the chocolate syrup after you add the hot shots of espresso to help blend the chocolate into the drink. Then add steamed milk. Stir again. A mocha is usually topped with whip cream.

Iced Mochas or Lattes: The process for preparing an iced latte or mocha is the same as preparing a hot drink, except that after the syrup and coffee are added you then add a scoop of ice, pour cold milk over that, and stir well.

Cappuccino: A cappuccino is a latte with extra foam. A wet or dry cappuccino specifies the amount of foam used from the steamed milk. A wet cappuccino is usually split into 3 equal parts: coffee, steamed milk and foam. The top third of the drink is filled with thick foam. A dry cappuccino consists of coffee and the rest foam. You will feel as if you are serving a cup of air. To create excess foam in the steaming process, just perform the foaming process where you inject air at the surface of the milk. Do not perform the blending process. Tap the pitcher on counter and spoon foam out into drink; do not pour any steamed milk into the drink, only foam.

This is a basic guide on drink preparation. Make sure that you have proper training. Familiarize yourself with your menu, equipment, and drink preparation process before serving your customers. You cannot afford to lose customers in the beginning from improper drink preparation or inefficiency.

Chapter 6

Hiring and managing employees

In my experience the best employees are college students. They are reliable, usually dependent on the money, young and appealing. A hiring system that has been successful for me has been to only hire people that know people that I know. I can not stress enough to stay away from hiring friends and family. The only exception would be your own children, because you are already in an authoritative position with them. Hiring children, family, and friends could create an unfair advantage with your other employees, as your relatives and friends might seem to receive special treatment. No matter who the employee, I would recommend having each one enter into an employee contract. That way there is no question as to what is expected of them. Below is a sample of the employee contract that I use.

Employment Contract
1. Treat each customer like a friend. Give them the best drink and customer service that they have ever had. Our #1 goal is great customer service and quality drinks.
2. Work together as a team in a team environment! Be willing to communicate any questions or concerns to the owners, not to other employees. Keep the lines of communication open, as I will do the same for you if I have any questions or concerns.
3. No discounts or free drinks to anyone. Immediate family members of each employee can have a $1.00 discount on their drink. (for example, mother, father, grandma, brother, etc.)

4. Be on time for your shift. If you are not able to work your scheduled shift because of illness or an emergency, please contact the owners immediately so that your shift can be covered.
5. Be willing to be flexible with your schedule as long as it does not interfere with your school schedule or other planned personal commitments, as the schedule may change from week to week.
6. Days off must be requested at least one week in advance.
7. Please limit personal phone calls and phone usage.
8. Any suspicion of theft is immediate grounds for termination.
9. Excessive customer complaints are immediate grounds for termination.
10. Unless prior approval is given, no one else is allowed inside the stand while you are working (such as friends or relatives).

By signing this document I agree to the guidelines set forth by the owner of the (Name of your business) effective upon hiring. I understand that not following these guidelines could result in disciplinary action including termination of employment.

_____
Employee signature   Date

Scheduling and staffing:
	Properly staffing your drive through stand is critical. There should be at least two workers in the morning, as you will do more than half of your business in the first five hours after opening. If you can not get the customers in and out in a timely manner and other cars are waiting in line you will lose business. Cars will drive by if the line is too long and go to the next available drive through. Once you build up a reliable customer base and learn your customers' drinks, the lines will move faster. You can look ahead to the next car and see what drink comes next.

Secret shoppers
	One tool that I use to evaluate my employee's ongoing performance is a secret shopper checklist. I have friends, family, or customers come through and complete the following checklist. Using this checklist ensures that my employees are preparing drinks properly and providing excellent customer service. And if they are not than I have the feedback in hand to know what additional training they need. This has been an invaluable tool in my business. I would suggest using it once your business is up and running.

SECRET SHOPPER CHECKLIST FOR DAILY HABIT ESPRESSO

DATE_____ Time_____
Brief description of employee_____

_____

_____

Customer Service
1. How long did you wait in line?

2. Were you greeted promptly once you pulled up?

3. Was the greeting friendly (did they ask you how you are or what they could get for you)?

4. Did they hold a conversation with you when they weren't preparing your drink, or when they could talk to you? When steaming milk or grinding coffee we can't hear you, we try not to talk then.

5. Overall how would you rate the friendliness and attentiveness of this employee toward you. On a scale from 1-10 (10 being the highest).

Quality of Drink
1. Was the drink made the way that you ordered it? For example, you ordered it iced and it came hot or asked for it to be drinkable and it was extra hot.

2. Did the drink taste the way that you like it (more flavor, less flavor, coffee taste)?

3. Did your drink have foam on the top (unless you specifically asked for no foam)?

4. If you ordered a mocha or chocolate based drink, did they ask if you wanted whip cream?

Closing
1. Were you charged the correct price?

2. Were you asked if your drink tastes right or OK?

3. Were you asked if you would like a punch card?

4. Were you told thank you or Have a Nice Day?

Additional comments:

Chapter 7

Smooth Operating

Once you have followed all of the steps that have been outlined for you, your business will be in a great location. Your service will be efficient and friendly, and your drinks great. You are ready for success. Remember that the most successful drive through espresso stands are ones in which the owners have a hand in day to day operations. Staying on top of training, equipment maintenance, and customer service will prove rewarding both personally and financially. Best of Luck!

Chapter 8 Worksheets

Use the following worksheets to aid you in developing your business. Make copies if needed before marking on the originals.

Drive through espresso location checklist

- It is on the morning commuter traffic side of the street. Cars drive by it while going to work.

- There are 35,000 cars or more per day that drive on that street.

- It is close to a college, hospital, large housing development, or mall.

- It is easy for cars to enter into and exit out of the parking lot.

- It is a highly visible location. Not set back off of the main street or obstructed by other businesses or buildings.

- There is enough room to build a drive through stand and still have four cars at each window without cars blocking traffic.

- You can secure at least a five- year lease with the property owner at a monthly rent that is reasonable.

- You have contacted the city zoning department to ensure that it is properly zoned for drive through espresso and you can hook up to utilities.

New Employee Checklist

- ❏ The potential employee looks appealing, has a nice smile, sunny disposition.

- ❏ This person is in need of work not just working for a hobby or for something to occupy their time.

- ❏ The potential employee has prior experience as a barista or at least some experience in customer service, food handling, or serving.

- ❏ This person has reliable references and you have contacted their last employer and they have vouched for this person.

- ❏ This person has a flexible schedule and is willing to work a variety of shifts.

- ❏ Their résumé shows them as an outgoing individual, participating in extra circular activities, sports, camps, or volunteer work.

- ❏ You know someone personally that knows this person and can vouch for their character and personality.

Creating a business plan

When developing a business plan there are five fundamental things that investors and banks look for. They need to have presented to them
- A detailed description of the business that you are going to start
- The market that you are going to appeal to and how appealing that market is
- How you plan to develop and run your business
- The management in all aspects related to operating your own business
- Your financial stability and financial plan for running this business.

1. A business description is a detailed review of the type of business that you are going to start. Include specific details such as location, secured lease, how you are you going to stand above the competition, what skills you are going to bring to this new business, or how you are going to grow the existing customer base of one already operating.
2. Describe the drive through espresso market. What you will do to be successful in the drive through business. The location of your business and the customer base you will attract.
3. Describe the development and production plans of your business. Weather you are purchasing an existing business or building one from the ground up without the customers and employees in place include details such as purchase price, lease agreement, daily operating details, staffing, customer service, training. Reassure the lender that you have a clear plan on how you are going to start or take over this business.
4. Tell how you will manage the business. A lender wants to know that you are capable of managing every aspect of the business. This includes money management, customer relations, employees, and inventory. Include any experience that you have with managing or hiring employees, providing customer service, and ordering supplies.

Refer to your financial stability, include a personal net worth statement if it will help.
5. Explain the financial aspect of running your business. Here is where you will refer to your profit and loss statement that you have prepared based on the variables to fit your situation. If you are purchasing an existing business use the business' last years sales to get your projected daily sales amount. Show that the income the business produces monthly will cover all expenses. Mention any reserve money that you may have to show the ability to cover the loan payment from another source other than the business income.

Attach these additional statements if applicable
- Personal financial statement
- Cash flow statement
- Expected Profit and loss
- Purchase offer
- Lease agreement
- Sample blueprint

Sample Business Plan

Business Description

The coffee industry is a multi-billion dollar industry with the number of specialty coffee drinkers increasing rapidly every year. During the last seven years of business, operating a drive through espresso stand I have strived to offer superior products and service to my customers resulting in increased sales averaging 20% a year. My goal has always been to provide those specialty coffee drinkers with an exceptional product, and outstanding service at my establishment resulting in a loyal customer following and steady profits.

As a successful drive through espresso owner I wish to attain another espresso business and provide the same exceptional product and service that has proven to be successful. The business that I want to acquire has been in business over five years and has a successful track record of sales and profit however; the owner has been absent the last year due to a back injury and surgery, resulting in a slight sales decline. I would have a day to day hand in the operations and service, and raise sales back to their potential for this busy location. With a secured lease with the property owner for the term of three years and four months the term of the loan at three years, it would be a sound investment for the lender as well as myself to purchase this business. The price of the drive through is reflective of its profits in that the earnings ratio is 2.7. The loan would be paid in full before the lease agreement had expired. At the end of the lease term I would then hope to renew the lease.

The market

The specialty coffee market is the fastest growing sector of the coffee industry. New products and supplies are being introduced monthly, appealing to the growing market

In the last 6 years of business as a drive through owner, I have watched my sales steadily increase every year. Being involved in the daily operations of a thriving business, I know what it takes to capture a customer and keep them. I believe that consumers are becoming more educated on the preparation of espresso based drinks and they are demanding a properly prepared drink. I strive to give my customers the quality product that they have come to expect and love. I want to apply my business and customer service skills to capture those customers that are expecting a superior product and keep them.

I believe that I have been successful in the drive through business because of my work ethic and business skills. I have been in customer service for the last 14 years and I offer superior customer service, and train my employees to do the same. We have an edge over the competition in many ways. We learn customer's names, remember their regular drinks, send them Christmas cards and offer consistently friendly service. Also with over six years of experience in drink preparation and continued training we put out a superior and consistent product. Where the competition is failing is they don't have a hand in daily operations and rely on in-properly or unmotivated employees to run their business. Some are very new to the industry and have had little or no training and therefore their customers are used as guinea pigs, with a bad first impression they don't come back. Again customers are becoming well educated on what goes into making a great espresso based drink and they expect that quality every time, as they should. Because of the product and service that my drive through offers we have been successful in gaining a very loyal customer base.

Development and Production

The drive through business that I want to buy is in an ideal location. The purchase price for this business is $65,000.00. We have signed a buy sell agreement contingent on obtaining financing and re negotiating the lease with the land owner. My strategy in purchasing this business would be to take it over in a quiet manner, leaving the existing employees in place, and incorporating myself into working with the customers. The reason for this is; the business is already being run properly and the existing employees have built the clientele base. The customers are familiar with these employees and have a loyal following with them. I will improve upon the service and product already offered retaining the existing customer base, adding to it by overseeing daily operations and offering my expertise in drink preparation and customer service.

Management

    I feel that my money management skills are exceptional. I am not a risk taker and I research my investments thoroughly. At a very young age I have grasped the concept of money management and have applied it to work for me to generate a substantial personal net worth. I have always done my own payroll, record keeping, bookkeeping, and quarterly taxes. I keep a close watch on inventory, and cost of goods sold to ensure costs are staying low, generating a larger profit and ensuring there is no employee theft.

    I have over 10 years of experience in management. I feel that I have exceptional managerial skills with my employees. I have had wonderful employees, many of them returning to work for me after going into the "real world" work force. I mostly hire college students and they stay with my through their college years, some of them as long as four or five years. I treat my employees with respect and value their thoughts and ideas, I build a relationship with each employee getting to know them personally as well as professionally, this has proved wise for me in that they genuinely care about my business. I offer continue training and support to every employee so that they can excel, resulting in my business being a success.

Financial

   The risks involved with furnishing this loan are slim. This business has been established for over five years with a successful track record of profit. I have successfully operated the same kind of business for six years with a successful track record. My work ethic, money management and customer service skills make my business successful and I plan to apply those same skills to run this new business.

   I have outstanding credit and significant net worth. As you will see by the attached profit and loss statement this business will generate the income needed to furnish the loan payments, as well as provide me with additional income. My personal cash reserves offer a secondary payment source for this loan, and my existing business that is paid for in full offers the collateral that may be necessary to cover the loan amount over the value of the assets. My source of income from my other espresso stand is my sole source of income. For the last two years I have only been scheduled 12-20 hours per week, and the business still generates enough revenue to pay my salary stated on my financial statement. I would have a lot of time and energy to contribute to this new business without sacrificing my income from my existing business. Purchasing this business would be a sound investment and I would appreciate the funding to make this purchase possible.

   Thank you for your time and effort. I look forward to continued business with your financial institution.

Sincerely,

Brandi Graham